American Gestures

Alex Raffi

and

Richard L. Epstein

ARF

Advanced Reasoning Forum

Advanced Reasoning Forum
www.AdvancedReasoningForum.org
P.O. Box 635
Socorro, NM 87801
USA

paperback ISBN 978-1-938421-63-1

e-book pdf ISBN 978-1-938421-64-8

TABLE of CONTENTS

Introduction

These are the most commonly used American gestures, ones understood throughout the United States. We've included only gestures whose meaning is symbolic, not ones that are universal expressions of emotion, such as fear.

Phrases in quotation marks are said with the gesture or are the exact verbal equivalents of the gesture.

Phrases in parentheses are the explanation of what is meant.

Fists are always made with the thumb outside the fingers.

The sign + indicates successive parts of a gesture.

Common
Gestures

1. "Hello."

2. "Goodbye."

1. "Hello"

2. "Goodbye"

1. "Here I am."

2. "Please call on me."

3. "Help, please."

1. "Here I am."

2. "Please call on me."

3. "Help, stop please."

1. (Introduction)

2. (Greeting—
   hello or goodbye)

3. "It's a deal."
   (Agree on a contract.)

(Strong grasp from men.
Firm but not strong grasp from women.
Weak grasp is considered unpleasant.)

It is not common to hug or kiss.
This is called "Shaking hands."

1. (Introduction)

2. (Greeting—hello or goodbye)

3. "It's a deal."

"After you."

"Good kid."

"Hey, kid."

A friendly greeting.

(You're getting fat.)

A friendly greeting.

1. "Give me 5!"
   (Greeting.)

2. "All right!"
   (Celebration.
      That's great.)

The gesture is always returned.
When done at shoulder level it's a "High 5".

1. (Greeting)

2. (Celebration)

1. "Howdy."
   (Greeting at a distance.)

2. "Come here."
   "Come on this way."

1. "Howdy."

2. "Come here." "Come on this way."

"Call me."

"Let's talk (on the phone)."

(Blowing a kiss. Usually done at parting.)

"How about a ride?"

(Hitchhiking)

"Come here."

(Used to a friend, or when you want to entice someone to come.)

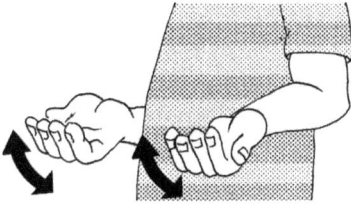

"Closer."

"A little closer."

"Come on."

Move just the fingers.

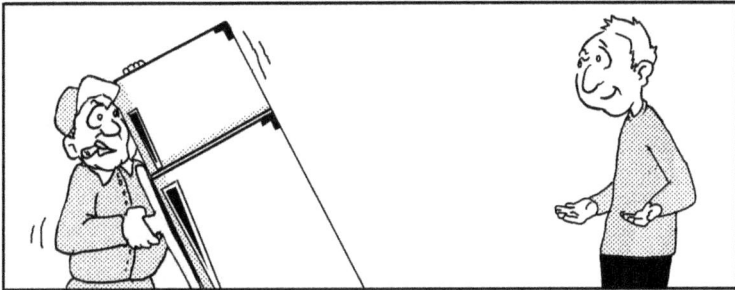

1. "Come here."
   (A sexual
   invitation.)

2. "Did you get it?"
   (I'm joking.)

This gesture is called a "Wink".

1. (A sexual invitation.)

2. (I'm joking.)

NOT POLITE

"What a babe!"

"Wow!"

"Look at that build."

"Check her out."

(She's really sexy.)

This is often accompanied by a "Wolf whistle" :

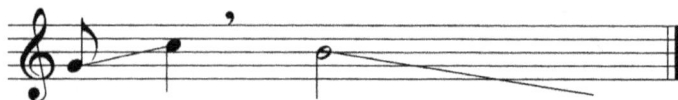

(The whistle is sometimes used by itself to attract a girl's attention.)

"She's pregnant"

NOT POLITE

"I'm kidding."

"I'm ribbing you."

"Look at that!"

"Shut up."

"Shhhh."

1. (Keep it a secret.)

2. (Be quiet.)

2. (Keep it a secret.)

2. (Be quiet.)

"She (he) is asleep."

"Cross my heart!"
"Cross my heart and hope to die!"
(I swear it's true.)

"I swear."

1. (On my honor it's true.)

2. (Taking an oath.)

Always done with the right hand.

1. (On my honor it's true.)

2. (Taking an oath.)

(Saluting the flag.)

(Begging.)

This is called
"Asking for a handout."

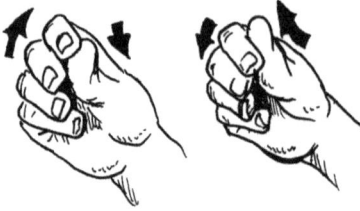

"Money."

NOT POLITE

(I want more money.   Money is the motive.
He/she has money.)

(Imitating a homosexual man.)

NOT POLITE

1. "Slow down." "Whoa."

2. "Back off." "Calm down."

3. "Hold it."

4. "Be seated."

1. "Slow down."

2. "Calm down." "Hold on."

3. "Hold it."

4. "Be seated."

"Look out."

"Watch out."

"No way."

(I will not be moved.
I will not change my mind.)

NOT POLITE

"Nobody here but us chickens."

(Whistle—no tune. Pretend to be innocent, when you know the other person won't believe you.)

"Bad, bad."

(Usually to a
child or animal)

NOT POLITE

"Oops."

(I made a mistake.)

NOT POLITE

"How did I get stuck
with such an idiot?"

"How can anyone
be so dumb?"

1. "I'm up to here with you."
   "I'm fed up."

   (I can't tolerate more
   of what you're doing.)

2. "I'm full."
   (I can't eat any more.)

1. "I'm fed up."

2. "I'm full."

- -

"I'm fed up!"

(I'm irritated to the very limit.)

NOT POLITE

"Nyahh, nyahh, nyahh, nyahh."

(Often silent, usually by children. Aggressive.)

NOT POLITE

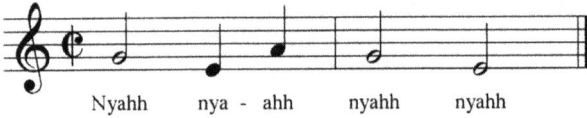

Nyahh   nya - ahh   nyahh   nyahh

"Nyahh, nyahh, nyahh, nyahh."

"Nyahh, nyahh, nyahh, nyahh."

"You son of a bitch!"

(Ready to fight.)

NOT POLITE

This gesture is called "Shaking your fist at someone".

"Don't push me."

(I'm getting angry, so you better stop. I'll get even.)

"I surrender."

"I give up."

"Time out."

(Stop. Allow time to cool off.)

Repeat the gesture 3 times.

This gesture comes from sports like football and basketball.

"What's the time?"

(Usually silent. Pretend to point at a wrist-watch.)

"Time's up."

"Cut it short."

(You're out of time.)

"Just a sec."
(sec = second)

"Just a minute."

"Give me a minute."

(Impatient waiting.)

This gesture is called "Tapping your foot."

NOT POLITE

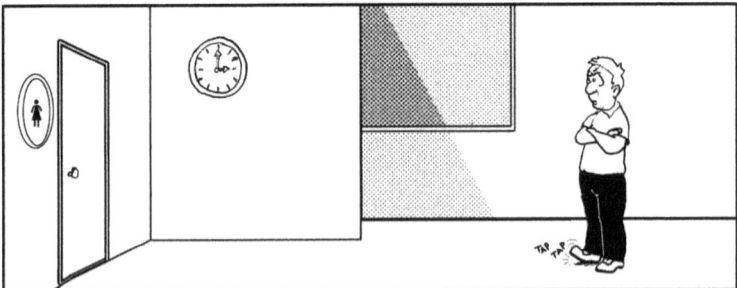

(I've got nothing to do, and I'm doing this because I'm bored and have to wait.)

This gesture is called "Twiddling your thumbs."

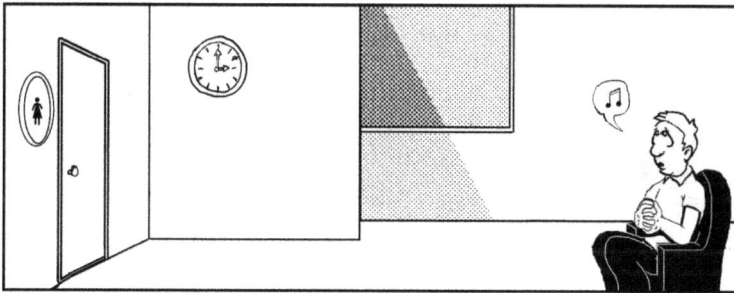

"Waiter—come here."

"Waiter—the check please."
(As if writing in the air.)

"Here's looking at you."

"Cheers."

"Here's mud in your eye."

"Here's to your health."

This is normally done when almost everyone has an alcoholic drink.

"Ahhhh."

(Contented.)

"Ohhhh."

(I ate too much.)

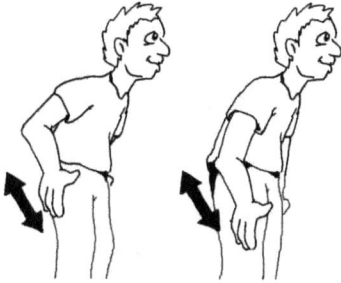

"All right, let's get down to work."

(Wipe hands on the sides of your pants as if your palms are sweaty.)

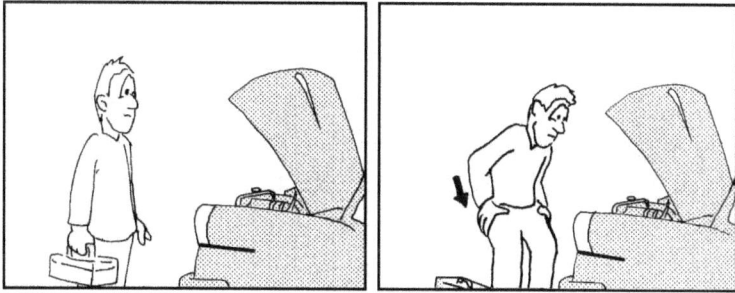

"All right, let's get down to work."

"That's that."

(That's the end of that job or problem.)

Slap your hands as if you're dusting them off.

This gesture is called
"Wiping your hands of the matter."

"Whew"

1. "That was close."

2. (I'm glad that's over.)

1. "That was close."

2. (I'm glad that's over.)

"Hmmm."

(Thinking hard, puzzled.)

"Hmmm."

(Thinking hard, puzzled.)

(Thinking.)

This gesture is called "Arms akimbo".

"Let me think."

"Blast!"

"Oh, no!"

(I forgot.)

"Blast!"

"Oh, no!"

(I forgot.)

"Blast!"

"Oh, no!"

(I forgot.)

1. "Darn it!"
   "Blast!"

2. "That's it!"
   "I've got it!"
   (I've got the idea.)

This is called "Snapping your fingers."

1. "Darn it!"

2. "That's it!" (I've got the idea.)

"P'-k'-tchew"

(I blew it. I did myself in. =
I just realized that I made a terrible mistake.)

This gesture is called "Shooting yourself in the head."

"Damn!"

(Greatly irritated at yourself.)

"Get out of here!"

(1. Pleased, but
embarrassed—
it's too much.)

(2. That's ridiculous.)

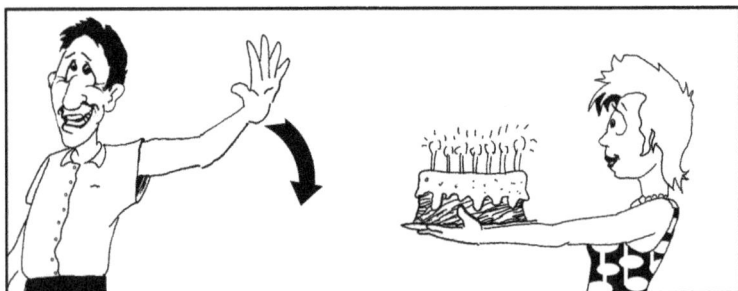

1. (Pleased but embarrassed.)

2. (That's ridiculous.)

"Aw shucks." (slang)

(Like a little boy embarrassed.)

"Beats me."

(I don't know.)

This gesture is called "Shrugging your shoulders".

1. "Who me?"
   "Moi?" ("Mwah"?)

2. "Not me!"

1. "Who me?"

2. "Not me!"

NOT POLITE

"Phyoo!"

("That went right over my head" =
It was too difficult to understand.)

"Whyoo!"

(Turn head very fast.)

"That went too fast for me to understand",
"I didn't catch that" = an idea,what he or she said
went by too fast for me to understand.

"What was that?"

"Come again?"

"Louder, please."

(I didn't hear you.)

"That's odd."

"He's crazy."

(Often just a nervous habit. When you pretend to bite your fingernails it tells someone you're anxious.)

NOT POLITE

"Fingers crossed."

1. "Good luck."
   (I hope this turns out O.K.)

2. (It doesn't count that I'm
   not telling the truth. —
   Usually by children.)

1. "Good luck."

2. (It doesn't count that I'm not telling the truth.)

"Please let it be."

(Praying.)

"Thumbs down."

(That's no good.)

"O.K."

"Got it."

"Thumbs up."

(That's right. I understand. Agreed. Good job.)

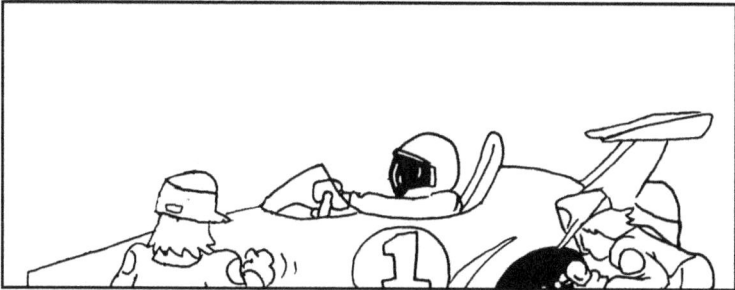

1. "Got 'cha."
   (Thanks—we did it
   with your help.)

2. (I finished that off.)

Click tongue (as if shooting).

1. "Got'cha." (Got you. Thanks.)

2. (I finished that off.)

"All right!"

(That's great!)

"All right!"

(That's great!)

This is more emphatic than the previous gesture.

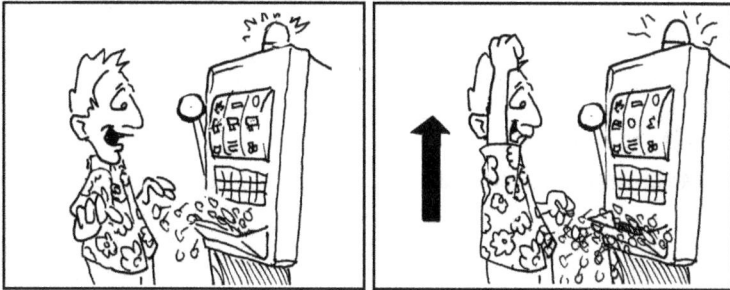

 +

"The winner!"

(Dejected)

"That's O.K."

"There, there."

Reassuring. Pat the shoulder two or three times.

"Good job."

(You did O.K. and deserve a compliment.)

Repeat 2 or 3 times.

This gesture is called giving someone "A pat on the back."

+

+

(I did a great job./ I'll congratulate myself.)

This is called "Patting yourself on the back."

NOT POLITE

(I'm great.
I did great.)

Pretend to polish
your nails.

(Aren't I great?)

Without a coat just pretend to hold out your lapels.

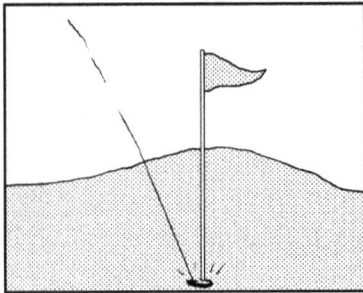

(Showing off how
strong or great you are.)

"Quotes."

What's said is really in quotation marks—
an actual quote from someone,
or you're not to be taken literally.

"I used my head."

"It's all up here."

(I used my intelligence.)

Tap two or three times.

"Perfect!"

"A–O.K."

(Great. Perfect.)

"A little bit."

"Just a bit."

"This big."

"Are you putting me on?"

"You must be joking."

(I don't believe you.)

Pretend to look over eyeglasses.

"Whoop Dee Doo."

"Whee."

"Whoopee."

NOT POLITE

(Sarcastic—it's not as important as you think.)

"Big deal."

(Sarcastic—it's not as important as you think.)

Move your hand three times.

NOT POLITE

"Boy are you hot!"

Lick your finger, then make a sound like steam. Usually sarcastic: the person touched is *so* hot, famous, important.

NOT POLITE

"She's (he's) stuck up."

(Someone's conceited.)

NOT POLITE

"You stink."   "Pee yew." (slang)

(You did really badly.)

"That's one for me/you."

Lick your finger and pretend to make a mark in the air. Usually used when someone gets the better of someone else in a conversation.

This is sometimes called "Scoring a point".

Yes, No, and Pointing

1. "You."
   "You may speak."

2. "You!"
   "Stop that this instant."

3. "Ha, ha, ha."

This is called "Pointing".

It is **NOT POLITE** to point, except
to pick someone out in a class or lecture.

1. "You." "You may speak."

2. "You!" "Stop that this instant."
   NOT POLITE

3. "Ha, ha, ha."

NOT POLITE

"Yes."

Move head up and down 2 or 3 times.

This is called "Nodding your head 'yes'."

"No."

Move head side to side 2 or 3 times.

This is called "Shaking your head 'no'."

Impolite
Actions

Don't do these in public!

NOT POLITE

NOT POLITE

NOT POLITE

NOT POLITE

NOT POLITE

NOT POLITE

NOT POLITE

NOT POLITE

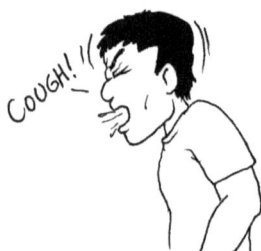

NOT POLITE

Cover your mouth!

NOT POLITE

NOT POLITE

Cover your face!

NOT POLITE

Don't eat where others
who aren't eating can't
avoid you.

NOT POLITE

NOT POLITE

NOT POLITE

Uncommon in public.
Lots of people find it
embarrassing. Don't
do this in a business
interview!

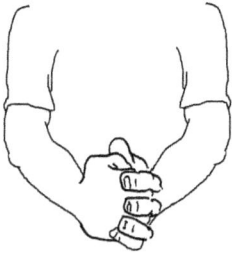

This is not a gesture!
It's just someone relaxing.

Obscene
Gestures

"He's jerking you off."

(He or she is a jerk. He or she is trying to make you believe something false or stupid.)

(Pretending to have sexual intercourse.)

"Fuck you!"

This is the most obscene gesture in the USA—
if you use this, be ready to fight.

This gesture is called "Giving someone the finger" or
"Flipping the bird".

Index

www.ingramcontent.com/pod-product-compliance
Lightning Source LLC
Chambersburg PA
CBHW060806050426
42449CB00008B/1564